Short And Imperfect Sketch Of The Blair Family

Dating Back Some Generations

Minnie B. Reynolds

Alpha Editions

This edition published in 2021

ISBN : 9789354416774

Design and Setting By
Alpha Editions
www.alphaedis.com
Email - info@alphaedis.com

As per information held with us this book is in Public Domain. This book is a reproduction of an important historical work. Alpha Editions uses the best technology to reproduce historical work in the same manner it was first published to preserve its original nature. Any marks or number seen are left intentionally to preserve its true form.

A Short and Imperfect Sketch of the Blair Family
Dating Back Some Generations.

> To the Kinfolks far and near,
>
> whose valuable help has made these records possible, greetings and thanks.
>
> Doubtless you will find errors not due to the printer, but these pages have been prepared faithfully and conscientiously with what data could be obtained.
>
> Be lenient and kindly in your judgment.
>
> May these records help to more closely bind into one great family all the descendants of the Blairs of Scotland.
>
> MRS. MINNIE B. REYNOLDS,
> *Historian.*

To the Friends and Relatives

who have the opportunity of obtaining this Genealogy, I have taken the liberty of extending our sincere appreciation for the untiring efforts of our Historian, who has made it possible for us all to have this valued record.

Without some one who was deeply interested and with no small amount of ambition, this could not have been brought about.

I am satisfied that in the years to come, this book will be a treasure in every household where owned.

Just a word in regard to the young men of the family who are in the service. It was impossible to obtain the names of them for our honor roll, but we are proud of you and may God care for you that you may return safely to those loved ones left behind who will back you to the finish.

    MERTON P. KNAPP,
        President.

Our native land was Scotland.

This land almost cut across by narrow and deep arms of the sea, with its many mountains, its towering cliffs, its stretches of gorse and heather developed a strong, independent, God-fearing people. From the natural features of the land the inhabitants were so separated that they differed in many ways, and in dialects. According to locality they were divided into Highland and Lowland Scotch. These great divisions were divided into clans, and again the clans were divided.

The Blairs belong to the Scotch Highlanders, to some division of a clan, but as the clan has not yet been determined, we cannot know our plaid.

In early Scotch history the Blair's figure largely, and in the wars which for a long time disrupted their land. In these wars they took a prominent part and are honorably mentioned. There was a Colonel Blair, a Blair Castle, and a Blair Coat of Arms.

Blair is a Celtic word which means a cleared field.

The Blairs of Scotland have always been prominent in civil and religious affairs, men of sterling worth, and their motto is: "I love proving or testing." We are proud of our heritage and will do well always to prove and test people and things and hold to the noble and the worthy, and reject all which tends to pull us down.

In all Scotch history we do not find a dishonorable or unworthy Blair, which emphasizes the value of the motto to all generations past, present and to come, to "Prove all things, hold fast that which is good." Our branch of the Blairs removed from Scotland to the north of Ireland in the early part of Cromwell's reign. They with other of their countrymen appear to have formed a colony retaining the peculiar religious and political views of their own country.

After about two years in Ireland, David Blair, with his wife and eleven children, in 1720 embarked for the American Colonies.

They arrived at Boston, Mass., the same year, and in a few months removed to Worcester County, which became their home.

The children of David, were Matthew, James, John, William, Robert, Joseph, Sarah, Dolly, Mary, Betsey and David.

According to dates, David must have been about forty years of age when he came to America. His children must have married and at the time of the Revolution, had sons of mature age to fight in this war. It is said, that one of the sons, John by name, who was a boy of seven years when he came to this country, later married an English lady, Ann Pepper. They had three sons in the Revolutionary War. Asa was shot in the leg in the battle of White Plains, but backing up to a fence he fired nine more times. He was recovering from his wound, in a hospital, when he was carried off by camp distemper.

His brother Joseph served through the Revolution. His brother James was a "Minute Man," kept his musket on the porch ready for use, also his knapsack, which his wife kept filled with fresh bread. Often he came from the field, seized musket and knapsack and was off without the loss of a moment.

Another son of this family was Aaron, a man of prodigious strength and size, and the only Blair of whom tradition speaks as a bachelor. Of the other children of John Blair, if there were any, we have no record. James of this family, was baptized in 1748 at Herdwicke, Mass., and in 1770, married Sarah Josslyn. They lived at Oakham, Mass., and there, with one exception, Joel, the names of his children are recorded.

The descendants of this James Blair we are able to trace with a reasonable degree of accuracy.

The children of James Blair: One, Joseph; two, Lucy, three, Sally; four, Asa; five, James; six, Katy; seven, Joel; eight, Hosea; nine, Polly; all born in Oakham, Mass.

Of these Joseph, Asa, Sally, Polly and Joel, lived most of their lives in New York State; James, Hosea and Lucy, who married a Mr. Rogers, in Canada; Katie married a Mr. Stone and lived in New Hampshire.

James Blair married the second time, the widow Hagar, a society woman, and given to pleasure.

One, Joseph, son of James Blair (m.) Polly Bouillard, whose father was a captain in the Revolutionary war. Their children were: One, Russell; two, Jason; three, Franklin; four, Sally; five, Adaline; six, Saphronia; seven, Lomira; eight, Seraph; nine, Roswell; ten, Joslin.

One, Russell, son of Joseph Blair (m.) *Mrs. Marie Smith, Their children were Charles Franklin (b.) 1836, Olean, N. Y., (d.) 1905, and William and Mary Blair.

*A grand daughter says her grandmother was Mrs. Marie Smith, other authorities say Polly Hager.

Charles Franklin Blair (m.) Elizabeth Ann Lyon, Keokuk, Ia., 1857. His occupation, merchant.

Their children were: George Reed (b.) 1858; two, Mary Saphronia (b.) 1861; three, Annie Belle (b.) 1863; four, John

Russell (b.) 1866, (d.) 1917; five, William Mudgett (b.) 1870; six, Harriet Luvisa (b.) 1874, (d.) 1878; all born in Iowa.

George Reed Blair (m.) Geneva Ashcraft, 1886, Saratoga, Kan. His occupation, retired farmer and bookkeeper. Home, 721 S. Oak Street, Pratt, Kan.

Their children are: One, Byron Ellsworth Blair (b.) 1887, graduate Pratt High School and State Agricultural College. He (m.) Lora K. Brown, 1914. His occupation, farmer. Home, Sawyer, Kan. Has one child, Portia Elizabeth Blair (b.) 1915; two, Mabel Ann (b.) 1890, (d.) 1891; three, daughter (b.) 1892, (d.) same day; four, Nettie Beatrice (b.) 1896, Sawyer, Kan. (m.) 1916, Ernest Roberts, Pratt, Kan.

Mary Saphronia, second child of Charles Franklin Blair (m.) 1882, John A. Floyd, dealer in lumber, grain and flour. Their children are: Ruth Irene (b.) 1883, Mary Elizabeth (b.) 1884, John Hunter (b.) 1886.

John A. Floyd (d.) 1887, and Mary S. Floyd (m.) 1896, H. A. Miller. Their children are: Hortense Antoinette (b.) 1897, Herbert Antone Miller (b.) 1902.

Ruth Irene Floyd (m.) W. E. Franck, 1901, Kansas City, Mo. One child, Ruth Isabel (b.) 1902, (d.) 1910.

Mary E. Floyd is physical director Y. W. C. A., Tampa, Fla.

John Hunter Floyd (m.) Alma Wusson, 1908. Their children are: Addison Hunter (b.) 1909, and Eugene Frederick (b.) 1912. John Hunter Floyds, home, Salina, Kan.; occupation, express messenger, U. P. R. R.

Three, Annie Belle Blair (m.) John P. Balmer, 1887, Saratoga, Kan. Occupation, retired stockman and farmer. Home, Pontiac, Ill., R. R. 5. Their children are: Annie Christine (b.) 1889, (d.) same week; two, Homer Blair (b.) 1891, (d.) 1892; three, John Everett (b.) 1893, (m.) 1917. Occupation, mechanic. Four, Angie Belle Balmer, (b.) 1895. Graduate Illinois Wesleyan Academy, now student in Illinois Wesleyan University, Bloomington, Ill.

John Russell, son of Charles Franklin Blair (m.) Mary Edna Miller, 1890. Occupation, jeweler and optician, Osage, Okla. Their children are: John Vance (b.) 1891, graduate Ph. G., Omaha, Neb., medical student, University of Oklahoma, Norman, Okla. Bruce William (b.) 1893, Big Mound, Ia. Occupation, barber, Eldorado, Okla.; Florence Nightengale (b.) 1894, Sawyer, Kan., graduate Cottey College Academy Nev., Mo., now student nurse in University of Oklahoma, Oklahoma City, Okla.

Francis Parkins (b.) 1900, Galesburg, Ill.

Fred Miller Blair (b.) 1909, Herrick, S. D.

William Mudgett, son of Charles Franklin Blair (m.) Jessie Wheat, 1903, Nezperce, Ida. Occupation, ranchman, Helena, Mont., Sta. 1.

Their children are: One, Viola Jessie (b.) 1904, Ilo, Ida.; two, Geneva Violet (b.) 1906; three, Stanley William (b.) 1911; four, Daughter (b.) 1913, (d.) same day.

This ends the record of Russell, son of Joseph Blair.

Two, Jason, son of Joseph Blair (b.) Massachusetts, 1810 (d.) 1913, (m.) Zeruiah Graves of Lisle, N. Y, 1835. They had seven children. Three died in infancy. Sarah (b.) 1838, (d.) 1865; Lovisa (b.) 1845, (m.) 1877; William H. Filer (d.) of Allegany, N. Y. They had two children: Grace E. (b) 1880, (m.) 1905, Ernest W. Potter. One son, Ralph Robert Potter.

The other child, Ralph Jason Filer, is unmarried.

Lovina Blair (b.) 1848, (m.) Charles McMall, 1868. They had five children, three living. Hattie, now Mrs. Charles Laube of Buffalo, N. Y.; May, Mrs. Daniel Jones of Buffalo, N. Y., and Ella McMall, an invalid.

Joseph C. Blair (b.) 1836, Allegany, N. Y., (m.) 1872, Mary Ellis. Their daughter, Marcia L. Blair, (m.) Cary C. Daniels of Perry, N. Y. They have one child, Reva Elizabeth (b.) 1909. In 1914 these Blairs and Daniels moved to Zephyrhills, Fla.

Three, Franklin, son of Joseph Blair (m.) Ruth Ann Bishop. They had eight children: One, Nathaniel, two, Lucy Amanda; three, Sarah; four, Julia; five, Joanna; six, Alice, seven, eight.

Nathaniel (m.) Elizabeth Smith. They had two children: Lillian, who married Walter Dorland, and Harry Nathaniel, who married Bertha Peck. Home of these, Skaneatelas, N. Y.

Sarah Julia Blair (d.) 1904, (m.) William Ely Ellis. They had four children: Hattie Belle (b.) 1864, (d.) 1881; Harry Frank (b.) 1869, (m.) Edith Hinsdale. Home, 30 Moffat Avenue, Binghamton, N. Y.

Willie B. (b.) about 1872, (d.) 1880.

Nathaniel J. Ellis (b.) 1878. Home in New York City.

Lucy Amanda and Alice Blair (d.)

Joanna Blair (m.) J. A. Lewis. She is the only living one of her father's family. Their children are: William C. who (m.) Florence Blaisdell, Edith (m.) George B. Morton. One child, Reva Morton, and Harry B. Lewis. All live, 167 Main Street, Binghamton, N. Y.

Four, Sally, oldest daughter of Joseph Blair (m.) Charles Atwater. They had two children, Harry (d.) 1913, aged 86 years; Franklin (d.) as a child. Harry had two children, Chester Atwater and Mrs. E. Halliday of Olean, N. Y. Charles Atwater (m.) second time, Saphronia, daughter of Joseph Blair. She died about 1883. Their children were: Adaline Eldredge (b.) 1883, (d.) ——; Marthy J. Harvey (b.) 1835, (d.) 1873; Isaac E. Atwater (b.) 1839, (d.) ——; David H. Atwater (b.) 1842, and Benjamin E. Atwater (b.) 1844. Home, in Alaska. Sarah L., now Mrs. S. L. Besecker, (b.) 1848; home, 1004 N. 17th Street, Boise, Ida. Charles J. Atwater (b.) 1852; home, Franklinville, N. Y. Mary P. Atwater (b.) 1832, (m.) William Swartz, who died in Civil War. Their children were: Omar E. (b.) 1852, Elva A. (b.) 1853, Ada (b.) 1856, Ida Jane (b.) 1858, and Elmer Warren Swartz (b.) 1854. Mrs. Mary P. Swartz (m.) the second time Daniel Bradford. One child: Charles Bradford, who died as a child. Address, Olean, N. Y.

Ida Jane Swartz (m.) 1877, Charles Edward Osgood. Their children are: Ethel Ruth Osgood (b.) 1878, Eleanor Ray (b.) 1879, Mable Clair (b.) 1882, Ruby May (b.) 1885, Benjamin Harrison (b.) 1888, Irena Pamelia (b.) 1891.

Eleanor Ray Osgood (m.) 1899, Merton Eldredge (d.) Their children are: Charles (b.) 1900, and Eleanor Eldredge (b.) 1905.

Mable Clair Osgood (m.) 1889, Frank Hill (d.) Their children are: Nellie Parmelia (b.) 1900, and Louise Frank Hill (b.) 1903.

Mable Clair Hill (m.) second time, Jacob Keobler, 1912.

Ruby May Osgood (m.) 1901, Joseph Warters. Their children are: Harry Frances (b.) 1902, and Evely Lucile Warters (b.) 1903. Mrs. Ruby May Warters is a nurse. Address, Olean, N. Y., R. R. 2.

Benjamin Harrison Osgood (m.) 1912, Nellie Byrons. One child, Wilson Osgood (b.) 1914.

Omar E. Swartz (b.) 1852, (m.) 1877, Rosetta Keesler, (d.) Their children: Alice (b.) 1879; Abram (b.) 1885, (d.) 1913; Howard Swartz (b.) 1887, (d.) 1895.

Omar E. Swartz (m.) second time, Katherine Skiver, 1896. Their children: Helen F. (b.) 1897, Muriel Lee Swartz (b.) 1899, (d.) ——.

Elva A., daughter of Mary P. Atwater and William Swartz (m.) James F. Keesler, 1880. Their children are: James E. (b.) 1881, George W. (b.) 1889, Mildred C. (b.) 1890, Ward E. (b.) 1893, and Estella R. Keesler (b.) 1896.

Five, Adaline, daughter of Joseph Blair (m.) Benjamin Dennison. Their children were: Alfred (d.) 1917, (m.) Miss Bartholomew. They had two sons and a daughter (d.), Joseph, Genie and Vergie Dennison. Virgie (m.) Mr. Willis, and lives in Binghamton, N. Y.

Seven, Lomira, daughter of Joseph Blair (m.) Charles Graves.

Eight, Seraph Blair (m.) Nate Horton. Two children: Eva and a son.

Nine. Roswell, son of Joseph Blair (m.) Mariette Shaler. Their children: George, who died in California, a veteran of the Civil War, Olive (m.) Mr. Cooper and (d.) in Springfield, Pa., Benjamin, a veteran of the Civil War (d.) 1917, (m.) Catherine Maria Cooper. Home, Union, N. Y. Their children: Cora E. (m.) Stephen Ulrick. Home, Campville, N. Y. Their children: Margaret (m.) Ray Winters, home, Cincinnati, O.; Benjamin D. (d.) aged 19 years; Reta (m.) Charles Dombert. The Dombert children are: Clifford and Esther. Catherine Ulrick (m.) Fred Mills. Leo Ulrick, now 1916, on Mexican border, and Fred Ulrick, who lives home.

Vina Blair (m.) Martin Holden, of Union, N. Y. Their children are: Beulah and Leslie living, Benjamin and Teressa dead.

Elsie Blair (m.) Percy Bidwell. Their children are: Richard and Lewis Bidwell. Home, Johnson City, N. Y.

Jimmie Blair (m.) Lena Bills. One child, Isabella Blair.

Benjamin Blair had another son, James, who died as a child.

Francis, son of Roswell Blair (d.) as a child. Theron (d.) was a veteran of the Civil War. Julia (m.) M. C. McCarrick. Home, Smithville Flats, N. Y.

Eugene Blair (m.) Lucinda Canfield. Their children are: Julia, Freddie and Henry Blair. Home, Paterson, N. J.

Rose Blair (m.) Lewis Leonard. Their children: Robert and Alvin Leonard, of Sayre, Pa., and Laban and Ella Mae Leonard, who live with their parents at Spencer, N. Y.

Ten, Joslin (b.) 1820, son of Joseph Blair (m.) Jerusha Hamlin. He died 1912. Their children were: One, Charles Henry (d.) as a child; two, Francis A.; three, Dwight (d.) aged about 21 years; four, Addie; five, Jennie; six, Seth (d.) as a child, and Celia Blair.

Francis A. Blair (m.) Frankie Hoadley. Two children: Pearl and Lena Blair.

Pearl (m.) Henry Greenman. Home, Rochester, N. Y. One child, Roger Greenman, Jr.

Lena Blair (m.) Frank Bell. Home, Groton Avenue, Cortland, N. Y. Their children are: Olive J. Bell (m.) G. H. Pifer. Home, Rochester, N. Y. One child, Esther Adalaide Pifer. Roswell P. Bell has a son, Roswell P., Jr. M. Le Vier Bell, Gertrude Blair, Lullus Donald, Ru Wet Myles, and Vivien Christene Bell.

Addie Blair (m.) Jerome Pollard (d.) They had a daughter, Jennie Pollard. Addie Blair Pollard's second husband was Alson Allen (d.) Their children were: Karl Pollard and Carroll Blair Allen. All live at 759 Ostrom Avenue, Syracuse, N. Y.

Jennie Blair (m.) Charles Wheeler. Two children, George Wheeler who married Edith Teeter. One child Aliene Teeter, and Eva Blair Wheeler (m.) Louie Monroe. One child: Dorcas Monroe. Home, 12 Broadway, Cortland, N. Y.

Celia Blair (m.) Dudley Wightman. Their children are: Burrill, Clair, Mildred, Harry and Arleine Wightman. Home, Marathon, R. D.

Sally, daughter of James Blair (b.) 1772, (m.) 1793, George Black, both born in Oakham, Mass. George (d.) 1810, and Sally, 1863. Their children were: James W., Elizabeth C., Sherlock F., Sally J., Isabell, Lucy and George W. Black.

James W. (b.) 1794, (m.) Deborah Bigelow. Had two sons, George W. and Christopher C. in United States service. He died about 1863, unmarried. Elizabeth C. (b.) 1796, (m.) William Chase, 1818, (d.) 1880. No children.

Sherlock F. Black (b.) 1798, (d.) 1880, unmarried.

Sally Josslyn Black, (b.) 1800, (d.) 1868, (m.) Hosea Young, 1822. They lived a mile east of Castle Creek, N. Y., and their children were born there. Later they moved to Chilhowee, Me.

Their children were:

One, Aaron Winne (b.) 1822, (d.) 1890. Lawyer, unmarried.

Two, George Black (b.) 1825, (m.) Caroline Fox, 1858, (d.) 1876. He was an M. D.

Three, Elizabeth Mary (b.) 1826, (m.) Amasa Tucker, 1872, (d.) Houston, Tex., 1875.

Four, Lucy Louisa, (b.) 1829, (d.) 1875, unmarried.

Five, Hannah (b.) 1833, (m.) Enoch Barnum, 1862, (d.) Warrensburg, Mo., 1894. Their children were Marion Young (b.) 1866, (m.) Mary Donovan, 1890. They have one daughter married to Joseph E. Brewer, and the Brewers have a son Joseph.

The Barnums and Brewers live a Independance, Mo., R. R. 1, Box 9. The second child of Hannah Barnum was Sally Annette (b.) 1868; home, 3339 Wabash Avenue, Kansas City, Mo.

The third child of Hannah Barnum was Lucus Hosea Enoch Barnum (b.) 1877, (m.) Josephine Lightcap, 1899. Four children, two living, girl and boy. Home, Merriam, Johnson County, Kansas, R. R. 1, Box 182.

Six, Jonas Abram Young, (b.) 1836, (m.) Fannie E. Robinson, 1890. For many years he was a prosperous merchant in Chilhowee, Me., and he now has business interests in that state, but his home is in Williamsville, Vt.

Seven, Homer H. Young, (b.) 1841, (d.) 1900, unmarried.

Isabell Black, daughter of Sally Blair Black (b.) 1803, (m.) John Dunn, 1826. Their children were: Cornelia, James H., Sally, Cornelius, Mary, Edward, George and John Emerson.

Cornelia (m.) Lorenzo Blair, (d.) 1885. Their children were: Belle, Emerson, Dora, Freelon, Etta, Clinton. Belle, Clinton and Dora are dead. Emerson married, but had no children. Freelon Blair (m.) Elma Chrysler (d.) No children. His second wife was Mrs. Ray Suttle. Two children, Nina (d.) and Neva (m.) Ray Barton.

Lorenzo Blair's daughter Etta (m.) Merritt Holdredge. These descendants of Cornelia Dunn and Lorenzo Blair live at Maine and Union, N. Y.

James, son of Isabel Dunn (m.) Eliza Terry. Two children: Anna Belle and Cora May. Anna Bell (m.) Fred J. Mable. Home, 142 Hawley Street, Binghamton, N. Y. Their children are: Frederick Leon, Edna Belle, now Mrs. Roy T. Roberts, and Emily Elizabeth Mable.

Cora May Dunn (m.) Horace R. Mable. Home, 146 Hawley Street, Binghamton, N. Y.

Sally and Edward Dunn died young, and Emerson as a young man.

Cornelius Dunn (d.) 1910, (m.) Mariette Blair, 1854. Residence, Pine Street, Binghamton, N. Y. Their children were: Jennie, Eddie, Clarence, La Motte, Adah. Eddie, La Motte and Adah died as children. Clarence married Emma Bloom. One child, Ruth, who since her mother's death has lived with her grandmother Dunn.

Clarence's second wife is Margaret Crowley. They live in San Francisco, Cal.

Jennie Dunn has been for 44 years a prominent teacher in the Binghamton schools. This year retired on a pension.

Mary Dunn (m.) Dr. John Munsell. They had a son John (d.) who (m.) Letitia Springsteen. They had two children, Harry and Bertha Munsell. Mary Dunn Munsell (m.) the second time, David Brown (d.) The Munsells and Browns live at 44 Pine Street, Binghamton, N. Y.

George, son of John Dunn (m.) Sarah Thomas. One child, Mabel, who (m.) Dr. Eggleston (d.) They have a son, George Dunn Eggleston. Home, Binghamton, N. Y.

Lucy Black (b.) 1805, (d.) 1884, unmarried.

George W. Black, (b.) 1808, (m.) Lydia Eldredge, (d.) 1851. His wife died 1854. Their children were: Ransom, Eli, Lucy Jane, Harriett Ann, Sherlock Foster, Julia P. and Ellen Black. A daughter Sally died as a young woman, and Rhoda and Edward, as children.

Ransom Black, (d.), (m.) Phebe Ann Gritman. They had three daughters all of whom died in their youth.

Eli Black (d.), (m.) Elvira Monroe. Their children are: Henry E., Myrta P., Mary E., and Frank S. Black. Frank (m.) Minnie Love, and their children are Helen and Charles Black.

Myrta Black (m.) George McCullen. Two daughters, Edith and Mary McCullen.

Edith Black (m.) Wilbur Garrett. They have a son, Wilbur Garrett, Jr., who lives in Washington, D. C.

Mary Black (m.) W. H. Tompson. They live in Nashville, Tenn. The others of Eli Black's family live at Whitney Point, N. Y.

Lucy Jane Black (d.) (m.) Benjamin Atwater. Their children were: Lenora, Albert and Willie Atwater.

Harriet A. Black (d.), (m.) Will Wolcott. One daughter, Mary A., who married George Crosby. The Crosbys had a son Paul who died in Manilla, a member of the Thirteenth Regiment Wisconsin Volunteers. The Wolcotts live in Chicago.

Julia Black (d.), (m.) Albert Crandall. Their children, Harriet, May and Lucy Crandall. May (m.) Mr. Frosch. Their children are: May, Harry, Charles and Lena Frosch (d.)

Lucy Crandall (m.) Mr. Abbott. One child, May Abbott.

S. Foster, sixth child of George and Lydia Black, a soldier in our Civil War, and prisoner at Andersonville in 1869, (m.) Ann Harris. They have two daughters, Maud Ella and Lena Lucy Black. Maud Ella (m.) Herbert Moulton, 1889. Their children are Paul Douglas, who (m.) Edna M. Whitney, 1910. Two children, Frederick Douglas and George Bartle Moulton. Home, 8 Exchange Street, Binghamton, N. Y. Maud Ella Moulton's other children are: Ethel, Pauline, Ruth Aline, Hazel Louise (d.), and Foster Black Moulton.

Lena Lucy Black (m.) Rev. Ward W. Watrous, 1898. Their children are: Lois Mahala, May Lydia, Ward Weston, Ariel Ella (d.), 1907, John Bradford and Lena Elizabeth Watrous. Home, Newark Valley, N. Y.

Ellen L., daughter of George and Lydia Black (m.) Edward B. Barton, 1870, (d.) 1917. Their children are: Ernest Foster, (m.) Hattie E. Barton, 1893. Their children are: Clara E. (b.) 1895, Bernita (b.) 1896, Leona (b.) 1906, Gertrude Barton (b.) 1912. Clara E. (m.) George Atwood, 1914, a son, Elmer B. Atwood (b.) 1916.

Bernita Barton (m.) Robert Crawford, 1913. One son, Ralston B. Crawford, (b.) 1914. Jessie Fancher Barton (m.) Edna M. Twining, 1908. Address of the Bartons, 207 Main Street, Union, N. Y.

Edward B. Barton (d.) 1917.

Asa, son of James Blair, (b.) 1780, (d.) 1869, (m.) Mehettable Ludden, 1800. Their children were: One, Louisa; two, Almira; three, Asaph, who died in infancy; four, Eli; five, Asa Edson; six, Clarinda; seven, Lucy Ann; eight, Spencer.

Louisa (b.) 1801, (d.) 1846, (m.) Hugh Cunningham, (b.) 1775, and of Spencer, Mass. He died 1858. They married 1816. Their children were born in Barker, Broome County, N. Y.

One, John, (b.) 1818, (d.) 1886, (m.) Hannah Lily, (d.) 1889; no children.

Two, James, (b.) 1819, (d.) 1857; unmarried.

Three, Asa, (b.) 1822, (d.) 1883; unmarried.

Four, Dexter, (b.) 1835, (d.) ———, (m.) Sarah Abigal Alderman, 1850, at Castle Creek, N. Y.

Five, Sarah Louisa, (b.) 1831, (d.) same year.

Six, Palmer, (b.) 1832, (d.) 1863, in hospital near Jackson, Miss. Member of Thirty-first Iowa Regiment Infantry.

Seven, Margaret L., (b.) 1835, (d.) 1894, in Iowa, (m.) Hardin Seaman, 1880.

Eight, Hugh Harrison Cunningham, (b.) 1839, (m.) Emily Washburn, 1862. He was a soldier of the Civil War. Dexter, fourth son of Hugh and Louisa, with his wife, in 1850, moved to Anamosa, Ia. Their children were:

One, Sarah Louisa, (b.) 1852, (m.) Dr. George W. Van Zandt, Chicago, Ill., 1886. He died 1913. Two, Emily F., (b.) 1854; three, Ellen L., (b.) 1857, (m.) Wm. A. Ladd; four, Jerome Dexter, (b.) 1862, (m.) Gertrude Barnard; five, Hattie Amaret, (b.) 1870; six, Fred Judson, (b.) 1872, (m.) Marjorie L. Carkeet.

Ellen L., third daughter of Dexter Cunningham, (m.) Wm. A. Ladd, of West Chester, Pa., 1877. Their children are:

One, Penn Matlack, (b.) 1879, (m.) Rose Belknap.

Two, Mildred, (b.) 1881, (m.) John Uhr.

Three, Edith E., (b.) 1882, (m.) Charles Miller.

Four, Allen Dexter, (b.) 1884.

Five, Clayton W., (b.) 1885, (m.) Laura Frances.

Six, Fred Clement, (b.) 1887, (m.) Blanche Day.

Seven, Sue Davidson, (b.) 1889, (m.) Frank B. Schrader, 1917.

Eight, Orsemus W. Ladd, (b.) 1891, (m.) Elizabeth Christianson.

Nine, Samuel A. Ladd (b.) 1895.

Children of Penn Matlock Ladd are Wilma, who died in infancy, and Edward, (b.) 1908.

Mildred and John Uhr who married 1906, have one child, Dexter W. Uhr.

Fred Clement Ladd has a son, Charles Atwood Ladd.

Orsemus W. Ladd has a son, Carl William, and daughter, Mildred Fay.

Jerome Dexter, son of Dexter Cunningham, children are: Albertine, (b.) 1885; Clarence Seablom, (b.) 1909, (d.) 1912.

Fred Barnard, (b.) 1889, (d.) 1901.

Belle (b.) 1892, (m.) Irving Burnette, 1914.

Fred Judson, son of Dexter Cunningham, (d.) 1914. Had two children, Marjorie H. and Sarah Abigal.

Hugh Harrison, son of Hugh Cunningham, with his wife, went to Anamosa, Ia., to live. Their children are: Lena Margaret, (b.) 1865, (m.) Jay V. Ferris, 1885, have a son, Robert Cunningham Ferris, (b.) 1889. Home, Eskridge, Kan. Edith Pearl, (b.) 1867.

Hugh Harrison Cunningham, (b.) 1881, (m.) Sue Wright,

1902. Their children are: Hugh Harrison (the fourth), (b.) 1903; Palmer Wright, (b.) 1905, and William Armour Cunningham, (b.) 1909. All children and grandchildren of Hugh Harrison Cunningham, born in Anamosa, except William Armour, who was born in Eskridge, Kan., where they all live.

Two, Almira or Elmira Blair, (b.) 1804, (d.) 1874, (m.) James Irvin. Their children are: One, Silas B.; two, Mary Ann; three, Harriet; four, Clarinda; five, Lucy; six, Caroline; seven, Louisa; eight, Mehetabel; nine, Martin; ten, John; eleven, James Irwin.

Silas B. Irwin, (b.) 1822, (d.) 1911, (m.) Hannah Smalley. Their children: One, Elmer, died as a child; two, Loretta, who died as a child; three, William; four, Elmer; five, Frank; six, Jessie. William died in early manhood, married Lettie Adams, one child, Clara May, who married Fred Loomis. They have two children. Elmer married and died in early manhood. Frank married. His children are Jessie, Silas, William.

Jessie Irwin (b.) 1867, (m.) Charles Marsh. Their children are: Lelia Irwin, Eugene Irwin and Francis Irwin Marsh. Home, Decovah, Ia., and also the home of Silas Irwin.

Mary Ann Irvin (m.) Joseph Fuller. She died 1917. Quite a family of children. Her home was at Genoa Junction, Wis.

Harriet Irvin (m.) Nelson Wentworth. Home, Manterville, Minn.

Louisa (d.), (m.) David Darling. Lucy (d.), (m.) Elijah Briggs.

Clarinda (m.) Joel Watkins. John (m.) Miss Sage. Martin Irvin (m.) Miss Johnson. Of Elmira Blair Irvin's children, Harriet Irvin Wentworth and Martin Irvin are the only ones living.

Eli, son of Asa Blair was (b.) 1807 and (d.) 1887, (m.) Lodica Johnson 1833. Their children were: One, Elmira; two, Charles; three and four, Frances and Fannie; five, Louisa; six, Oscar; seven, Royal La Fayette; eight, Delmont; nine, Eva; ten, Libbie, who died in infancy.

One, Elmira (d.) daughter of Eli Blair (m.) 1854, Oscar Blair (d.) 1862. One child, Etta, (m.) Arthur Riley, 1884. Their children are: Vere (d.) who (m.) Mabel Walters. One child, Edna Mae Riley.

Etta Riley's other children are: Oscar (d.), Edna (d.), and Veva and Byron Riley who live at home, Maine, N. Y.

Elmira Blair, 1866, (m.) Hamilton Ellerson. One child, Dicie Ellerson, who (m.) Judd Bailey. The Bailey's have a daughter Ruth.

Elmira Blair Ellerson (d.) 1896.

Charles, son of Eli Blair (d.) as a young man 1852.

Fannie Blair (m.) 1868, Charles Lewis. One Child: Cora Lewis, who (m.) 1898, Frank Hinds. Home, 8 DeForest Street, Binghamton, N. Y. Fannie Lewis (d.) 1896.

Francis Blair was a physician, (m.) Lydia Newland. He died 1904. Two daughters, Marjorie and Elizabeth Blair.

Louisa Blair (m.) 1866, John Knapp. One son, Merton, who (m.) Adelaide Gulnac. They have two sons, John and Robert Knapp. All live at 21 Frederick Street, Binghamton, N. Y.

Oscar and Delmont Blair went to California to live many years ago. Oscar (d.) 1896, (m.) Kitty McQuaid. Home in California. One son, Delmont Blair.

Royal LaFayette Blair (m.) Frank Godspeed, 1882. Home, Castle Creek, N. Y.

Delmont E. Blair (m.) in California, Mary Smith. Their children are: George Oscar, Marth Ann, and Delmont E. Blair. In 1916 George Oscar Blair (m.) Myrtle Neitz.

Eva Blair (m.) 1875, Morris Goodspeed. Their children: Floy (m.) James Davidson, 1908. One child: Richard Davidson, (b.) 1915. Floyd Goodspeed (d.) Ina (m.) 1915, Dr. William Moffatt. Glen Goodspeed lives at home, 19½ Frederick Street, Binghamton, N. Y.

Asa Edson, son of Asa Blair, (b.) 1810, (d.) 1884, (m.) 1836, Caroline P. Pease, who (d.) 1869. Asa Edson was born in Brookfield, Mass., (m.) second time, Affie Slater. The children of Asa Edson and Caroline Blair were Mary Jane, Morris Pease, Harriet Ann, Helen Eugenia, Minnie Blanche, Adalaide who died in infancy, Lewis Pease, and Arthur Edson Blair.

Mary J. Blair (m.) 1860, Lucius W. Moody. Their children were: Lucius Wilbur who died in infancy, Charles Amadon noted journalist, and one of the editors of "Out West" (d.) 1910, Robert Orton, Frederick Stowell, Frances Miner, Arthur Blair and Mary Grace Moody.

Charles Amadon Moody m.) 1883, Jennie Darrow (d.). One child: Charles Darrow Moody, who died in infancy. Charles (m.) second time, Ella Ladd, 1887. Two sons, Wilbur Ladd, (b.) 1888. Home, corner Henrietta and Berryman Streets, Berkeley, Calif. Graham Blair Moody (b.) 1889, (m.) Amy MacLoughlin. Home, 6721 De Longpre Avenue Hollywood, Calif. Robert Orton Moody (m.) Agnes Claypole, 1903. He is a physician and is connected with the University of California at Berkeley, Calif. His home address is 2826 Garber Street, Berkeley, Calif.

Frederick Stowell Moody (b.) 1867, (m.) May Van Dorn, 1890. One child, Rutherford Van Dorn Moody. Frederick Moody (m.) the second time, Macie Andrew. Their children are: Frederick Stowell Moody and George Robert Moody. Home, 33 Fourth Street, Stamford, Conn.

Frances Miner Moody (b.) 1869, (m.) Grace Butler Mix (d.) He (m.) the second time, Lillian Paranteaux. He is a clergyman. Home in California.

Arthur Edson Blair Moody was (b.) 1871 or 2. He (m.) Julia Wilkie Downey. One son, Blair Moody. Home, Providence, R. I.

Mary Grace Moody, B. Sc., has been for years a teacher in the New Haven High School. Address, 199 Elm Street, West Haven, Conn.

Her mother, Mary Blair Moody, was the first woman graduate of the Buffalo Medical College, in which city she practiced medicine for many years. Then the family moved to New Haven, Conn., where she continued work in her chosen profession. Her present address is 2826 Garber Street, Berkeley, Calif.

Morris Pease, son of A. Edson Blair (b.) 1839, (d.) 1903, a veteran of the Civil War, (m.) Margaret Helen Ryan, 1863. She died 1907. Their children were: Edson Pease (b.) 1864, (d.) 1865; Carrie Pease Blair (b.) 1866, (d.) 1886, Normal School graduate and a teacher.

Kittie Hillman (b.) 1868, (d.) 1881, Helen Eugenia (b.) 1872, (d.) 1890; Anna E. (b.) 1878, (d.) 1881; Morris Pease Blair (b.) 1881, (m.) 1900; Dolly Kent of Windsor, N. Y. Their children are: Ella Margaret (b.) 1901, James Kent (b.) 1903, Louis LaFayette (b.) 1905, Morris Elmo (b.) 1907, Harold Raymond Blair (b.) 1913. Home, Macomber Street, Port Dickinson, N. Y.

Harriet A., daughter of Edson Blair (m.) Capt. Wm. H. Bristol, 1864. He (d.) 1912. He was a veteran of the Civil War. Their children are: Irving Blair Bristol (b.) 1866, (m.) Etta Jane Robinson. Their children are: Vivien Harriet (b.) 1887, (m.) Arthur Gordon Wilson, 1907. Home, Dansville, N. Y. Grace Lillian (b.) 1889, and William Everett Bristol (b.) 1891, (m.) Mary Edith Hanner, 1913. Home, Sacramento, Calif.

Irving B. Bristol has been a great factor in advancing the temperance movement throughout the United States, and is now a prominent Methodist Episcopal preacher at Santa Cruz, Calif.

The other son is Rev. Lucius Moody Bristol, Ph. D. (m.) Minnie Babcock. Address 6 Brockway Avenue, Morgantown, W. Va. They have two children: Loris and Wilma. At present he is connected with the University of Virginia. He is also author of a book on Sociology which is used as a textbook in some of our leading universities.

Helen E. Blair (m.) William E. Johnson, 1866. Their children were: Hettie, who died as a child, also Harold. Mary Gertrude lives with her mother at 40 Bigelow Street, Binghamton, N. Y.

Minnie Blanche Blair (m.) George Reynolds, 1890. Her home is 38 Bigelow Street, Binghamton, N. Y.

Lewis Pease Blair (d.) 1908, (m.) Mary Slater, 1874.

They had a son who died in infancy. He married for his second wife, Marian Bliven, 1907. He was a successful physician and surgeon.

Arthur Edson, son of Edson Blair (b.) 1855, (d.) 1890, (m.) Mary Lamb. Their children were: Ralph, who died as a babe, and Mabelle who married George Campbell. She died 1907. One child, Eleanore, who died in infancy.

Arthur Edson Blair, her father, was a physician.

The mother of these children of Edson Blair was a writer of some note, writing for several of the best periodicals and magazines under the pen name of "Waif Woodland."

Clarinda, sixth child of Asa Blair, (b.) 1815, (d.) 1870, (m.) Elijah Fergusen, 1832. Lived in Broome County, N. Y., many years, where all their children were born. Moved to California about 1855. Their children were Grace, (b.) 1833, died as a babe; One, Jane Louisa (b.) 1834, (d.) 1903; two, John (b.) 1836, (d.) 1903; three, Francis Elmira (b.) 1838, (d.) 1909; four, James (b.) 1840; five, Alfred (b.) 1842; six, Mehettable (b.) 1846, (d.) 1889, (m.) J. W. Major. No children.

Jane Louisa Fergusen (m.) Charles S. Pease. Their children were Philip, (b.) in New York State 1854, the others in California; Ella Louise (b.) 1856, Alice C. (b.) 1862, Alfred (b.) 1865, Charles Henry (b.) 1867, and Edward C. Pease (b.) 1869. His present address is Sonora, Tuolumne Co., Calif., and Grace Pease.

John Fergusen (m.) Rosalie Mock, 1873. Their children are: One, Benjamin Elijah (b.) 1873, (d.) 1894; two, Henry Leon (b.) 1874; three, Clarinda (b.) 1877, (d.) 1889; four, Jeannette (b.) 1879, (m.); five, Carl Maurice (b.) 1881, (d.) 1911; six, Edna Salome (b.) 1882, (d.) 1911; seven, Adele Judith (b.) 1885, (d.) 1898; eight, Charles Clark (b.) 1886, (d.) 1904; nine, a son who died in infancy; ten, Frank Leslie (b.) 1891; eleven, John Ariel (b.) 1892; twelve, Ruth Marion Fergusen (b.) 1894.

Frances Elmira Fergusen (m.) William Henry Booker, 1857. Their children are: Clara Louise (b.) 1858, (m.) John Meginty, 1886. They had a daughter, Almy Meginty. Ann Eliza (b.) 1861, (m.) Joseph A. Shipe, 1880. Their children are: Irene Elizabeth (b.) 1881, (m.) 1902, Joseph Arthur Laugel. Their children are: Ruth Marguerite and William Laugel.

Emma Francis Shipe (b.) 1882, (m.) John W. Engle, 1904. Their children are: Grace, William, Raymond, Erma, Esther and Marjorie Engle.

Margaret Iona Shipe (b.) 1884, (m.) Charles Wesley Renfro, 1905. Their children: Donald, Della, Eleanore and Bernice Renfro.

Clara Louise Shipe (b.) 1887, (m.) Arthur Louis Rouse, 1909.

William Arnold Shipe (b.) 1890.

Hettie Jane, daughter of Frances Booker (b.) 1863, (m.) George S. Taylor, 1890. Their children are: Leslie, Ernest and Lelia Taylor.

Albert Henry Booker (b.) 1865, (d.) 1887.

William Elijah Booker (b.) 1867, (m.) Mary Frances Gibbs, 1892.

James Thomas Booker (b.) 1869, (m.) Pearl Kemp, 1905. Their children are: Chester and James Booker.

Joseph Alfred Booker (b.) 1871, (m.) Etta Crocker. They have a daughter, Myrtle Booker, who (m.) Harry Hill, 1916.

Ephriam Fergusen Booker (b.) 1873, (m.) Eliza Rowe. Their children are: William and Raymond Booker.

Walter Warren Booker (b.) 1877, (m.) Annie L. Pope, 1896. He (d.) 1915.

Leslie Edward Booker (b.) 1879, (m.) Lottie Minners, 1909. Their children are: Robert and Pauline Booker.

James and Alfred Fergusen are the only living of Clarinda Blair Fergusen's children.

Lucy Ann, seventh child of Asa Blair, (b.) 1818, (m.) George Hamlin, (d.) 1905. Their children were: Asa (d.) 1890, m. Ella Watrous, 1878.

Elmira (m.) Mark Perigo, 1890, (d.) 1897.

Fremont Hamlin (m.) Jennie Sheets, 1883. One child, Blanche Hamlin. Home, Montrose, Pa., R. R.

Edson Hamlin (m.) Allie Rhinevault, 1877. Two children, Ethel and George Hamlin. Ethel (m.) Warren Eastman. Two children, Hyla and George Eastman. Home, Montrose, Pa.

George Hamlin (m.) Cecil Rummer. Home, S. Montrose, Pa.

Edson Hamlin's second wife was Linda Hilton (d.) His address, Montrose, Pa.

Estella, daughter of George Hamlin, (m.) Jacob Dimon, 1876. He is dead. Their children were: Lena Belle, (d.) aged one year, and Maud (b.) 1880, (d.) 1885. Estella Dimon (m.) 1918, D. D. Layton, address Springville, Pa.

Spencer, youngest child of Asa Blair, (b.) 1822, (d.) 1870, (m.) Maria Knapp, who died 1897. Their children were: Asa Edson (b.) 1845, (d.) 1902; Estella Irene, (b.) about 1847, (d.) when about eleven years of age, in California. These two born in New York State. Spencer went to California in the early gold days, and later sent for his wife, and still later for the children who made the journey by themselves. His children born in California. Iona Blair (b.) 1861, and George Franklin Blair (b.) 1865. Iona Blair (m.) Mr. Holland, and their children were: Arthur Blair Holland (b.) 1890, and (d.) the same year, and Eva Maria Holland (b.) 1895.

George Franklin Blair (m.) Gabrielle Bushaw (d.) Their children are: Iona May (b.) 1891; George Asa (b.) 1893, (d.) 1894; Earl Leslie (b.) 1894; Estella Irene (b.) 1897; Delia M. (b.) 1899; Spencer (b.) 1901; Mark Franklin (b.) 1902; Idabelle (b.) 1904; Gabriel S. Blair (b.) 1907. George Blair and family lived at Santa Rosa, California. Iona May Blair (m.) Bradley Goodnough and lives at Fresno, Calif. Have two daughters and a son.

Estella Irene Blair (m.) Arthur Stewart. Lives in Santa Clara, Calif. Has a daughter, Delia H. Blair, (m.) Jack Nelson, and lives in San Francisco, Calif. Since their mother's death, 1907, Idabelle and Gabriel S. Blair have lived with their aunt, Iona Holland, 507 A Street, Santa Rosa, Calif. George Blair lives in Tuolumne, Calif.

FAMILY OF JOEL SON OF JAMES A. BLAIR.

James Blair's son Joel (m.) Mahala Page, 1841. When their first baby Alfred, was a year old they moved to Schoharie County, N. Y., bringing all their worldly possessions in a one horse wagon. He took up a tract of land, built his house, raised a family of eleven children: One, Alfred; two, Adaline; three, Rowena; four, Alonzo; five, Winslow; six, Lorenzo; seven, Willis;

eight, Parley; nine, Oscar; ten, Mariette; eleven, Mahala. So wisely did he live and so carefully did he plan, that when he died at 49 years of age, he left his family well provided for.

One, Alfred Blair (b.) 1831, (d.) 1900, (m.) Charlotte Allen. Their children: One, Joel, who died as a child; two, Rowena, who lived to be 60 or more, (d.) 1915; three, Roseltha (b.) 1839, (m.) H. C. Stannard, 1865. Had one child, Lizzie, who (m.) Frank Japhet. Their children: Kenneth, Ivan and Hazel.

Four, Harlan Page Blair (b.) 1841, (m.) Lizzie Cochran, 1865, (d.) 1889. He was a Presbyterian minister, she was a physician. Their children were: Daisy, who first (m.) Harry Bogart, 1895, he (d.) 1909. In 1913 she (m.) Harry Hall. One child, Richard Blair Hall. They live in Binghamton, N. Y. Margene B. Blair is principal of the Johnson City High School. Home, 34 Floral Avenue, Binghamton, N. Y.

Five, Phebe Ellen (b.) 1844, (m.) Isaac Arnold, home in Missouri. Their children are: Henry, Lena, Matie, Carry and Lottie Arnold. There are several grandchildren.

Six, Euphemie (b.) 1846, (m.) J. H. Saddlemire. Had one son Marcus, who (m.) and has several children.

Seven, Charlotte Blair (b.) 1848, (m.) Charles Fuller, 1869. One child, Adah Fuller. Charlotte (d.) 1888.

Eight, John A. Blair (b.) 1850, (m.) 1872, Hattie Lounsberry (d.) 1874. One child.

Nine, Marcus A. Blair (b.) 1855, (m.) Arletta Lockwood, 1882, (d.) Their children: Iva R. (b.) 1884, died as babe; baby (d.) 1885; John A. Blair (b.) 1887, Marcus A. Jr. (b.) 1900. Marcus A. (m.) the second time Ida Witter, 1914. Marcus is a druggist at New Milford, Pa.

Ten, Orissa I. Blair (d.) as a child.

Eleven, Alfred Blair's son, Andrew Stryker, (b.) 1857, (m.) Delilah Japhet. He is a physician at Great Bend, Pa. Their children are: Lelia (b.) 1884, (m.) Zelous Osterhought; one child, Bernice Blair Osterhought (b.) 1916. Home, 7 Allen Street, Binghamton, N. Y.

Cecil D. (b.) 1886, and Karl Blair (b.) 1896.

Cecil D. Blair lives in Buffalo, N. Y. Cecil (m.) Lucy ———. One child, (b.) 1916, Ralph Andrew Blair.

The second child of Joel Blair was Adaline (m.) Ephriam Nickerson. They had no children, but adopted her brother's daughter Celia.

Three, Rowena Blair (m.) D. Nickerson. Six children, Althina, Adaline, Mariette, George, Grover and David Nickerson. Althina Nickerson (m.) Hiram Smith. Their children are: Perdita who (m.) Edwin P. Cook, and the Cook children are: Allie, Smith and Deland. Allie Cook (m.) Gerald L. Wood and they have two children: Everett and Nina Wood. Smith Cook (m.) Clara Brookhout.

Rhoena Smith, daughter of Althina Nickerson Smith (m.) George Richmond. Their children are: Nellie and Anna Mae Richmond. Nellie Richmond (m.) James Snider and Anna Smith (m.) Lewis Case. One child, Allen Case. Nellie Smith (m.) George Engle. Their children: Elva and Mary Engle. Elva Engle (m.) Leslie Van Wie. One child in 1916 aged about three years.

Adaline, daughter of Rowena Blair Nickerson (m.) Filo Burhans. Their children: Charles and May Burhans. Charles Burhans (m.) Cora Warner. The Burhans had a daughter Anna who (m.) Floyd Blakesley. A daughter, Adaline Blakesley.

May Burhans (m.) Harry Conklin. A son, Howard Conklin.

Mariette Nickerson (m.) Henry Haskin. Their children are: Leonard, George W., Bursley, Lillian, Belva (d.) and Stanley Haskin.

Leonard Haskin (m.) Myrtle Van Dyck.

George W. Haskin (m.) Julia E. Frost.

Bursley Haskin (m.) Grace Richmond. Two sons: Olin and Doyle Haskin.

Lillian Haskin (m.) Oscar Applebee.

Belva Haskin (m.) Palmer Bates. Their children: Lena M. (b.) 1905, Alton H. (b.) 1910.

Stanley Haskin unmarried.

George Nickerson (d.) unmarried.

Grover Nickerson (m.) Harriett Wood. A son, George Wood.

David Nickerson (m.) Lena Case. Their children: Verge, John and Roy Nickerson.

Verge Nickerson (m.) Marcia Rickard. They had a child Norma, aged about two and one-half years in 1916.

John Nickerson (m.) Miss Bogardus. One child, about two years of age 1917.

Alonzo, the fourth child of Joel Blair (m.)

They had two children, Ellen and Milo Blair. Ellen (m.) Asher Wooster. Their children are: Del, Hattie, Grace, Arthur and James Wooster. Arthur first (m.) Frank Lull (d.) and second, Libbie Hayes (d.) Milo Wooster lives at Triangle, N. Y.

Winslow, fifth child of Joel Blair (m.) Mary Dean. Their children are: Frances Augusta, Lucy Mahala, Joel and Asa Blair.

Frances Augusta (d.) 1916, (m.) P. M. Jenks. Home, San Diego, Calif. No children.

Lucy Mahala (m.) Wakeman Mathews (d.) One child, Stella Mathews (m.)

Lucy Mahala's second husband, T. D. Smith. Home, San Diego, Calif.

Joel Blair (m.) Mary Robbins, (d.) Their children: Guy, Eleanor and Eulalia.

Guy Blair (m.) Alberta Inman. One son, Clinton C. Blair. Home, Hillyard, Wash.

Eleanor Blair (m.) George D. Anderson. Eulalia Blair (m.) Alexander Anderson. One child. The Andersons live at Newell, Ia.

Joel Blair (m.) the second time, Mary Anderson. Two children: Bernice and Marjorie Blair. Home, Early, Ia., and Joel is editor of The Early News.

Asa, son of Winslow Blair, (m.) Mary Mead. Their children are: Earl, Charles, Henry, Elnora and Lorilla Blair. Earl Blair (m.) Ruby Taylor (d.) His second wife was Anna Chapman. One son, Kenneth Blair.

Charles Blair (m.) Ida Ayres of Berkshire, N. Y. Henry (m.) Erma Swartz (d.) Two children: Francis and Mary.

Elnora (m.) Mr. Rogers. Lorilla Blair lives with her parents, 53 Endicott Avenue, Johnson City, N. Y. Winslow Blair's children: Ida and Eva (d.) as children.

For Lorenzo, son of Joel Blair, see Dunn record.

Willis, son of Joel Blair (m.) and his wife (d.), leaving a daughter Celia. She was adopted by her aunt, Adaline Nickerson. She (m.) Hezekiah Goodfellow. Their children were: Carrie (d.), Dell, Myrtie (d.), Ferdinand, Sadie and Willis Goodfellow. Carrie (m.) Frank Knapp. Two children: Grace and Nina.

Grace Knapp (m.) Clarence Mead, and they have three children: Richard, Kenneth and Alice Mead. Nina Knapp (m.) Clinton Marine. Two children: Donald and Roland Marine.

Dell Goodfellow (m.) George Knapp. They have three children: Iva (d.), Hazel and Claud. Hazel Knapp (m.) Norman A. Darion. Two children, Norman Russell and Marian Elizabeth Darion. Claude Knapp unmarried and lives at home. Dell Goodfellow Knapp's second husband, was Irving Woodward.

Ferdinand Goodfellow (m.) Florence Cameron.

Sadie Goodfellow (m.) James S. Lewis. A son, Wesley K. Lewis. Home, Syracuse, N. Y.

Willis Goodfellow (m.) Charlotte Smith. Three children: Douglas, Harold and Elizabeth Goodfellow.

Willis Blair (m.) the second time Diantha Knapp. One child, Della Blair, who (m.) Charles Emens. Four sons: Glen and Allen who died as young men, Fred who (m.) and lives in Owego, N. Y., and Harry Emens who (m.) Adeline Cooley. One son. Home, Ilion, N. Y. Mr. and Mrs. Charles Emens have recently gone to Marathon to live.

Parley, son of Joel Blair (m.) Phebe Dean. Nine children: Libbie (d.), Alice, Ida, Emma, Hattie, Luella, Charles (d.), Loren (d.) and Willie (d.).

Libbie (m.) Julius Bowen, 1867, (d.) 1893. Their children are: Minnie (d.) 1898, Oscar and Lena Bowen. Minnie Bowen (m.) George C. Taft, 1885. Their children are: Harvey D. (b.) 1886, John W. (b.) 1887, Hazel (b.) 1889, Ithel J. (b.) 1890, Oscar B. (b.) 1893, and Elizabeth M. Taft (b.) 1896.

George Oscar Bowen (m.) Nina J. McCarthy, 1903. He is musical director in the schools at Yonkers, N. Y., where they live.

Lena R. Bowen (m.) Frederick McNeal, 1914. Home, Chicago, Ill. Winter home, Ormond, Fla.

Alice Blair (m.) Edwin Huntley, 1870. They have two sons: Charles and Floyd Huntley. Charles Huntley (m.) Addie McDowell, 1892. Their children are: Genevere (b.) 1895, Lester (b.) 1900, Alta Huntley (b.) 1911. Home, Harpursville, N. Y.

Floyd Huntley (m.) Susie Davis, 1900. Their children are: Myrtle May (b.) 1904, Mildred (b.) 1906, William (b.) 1911, Alice (b.) 1913, and Floyd Huntley, Jr., (b.) 1915. Home, Whitney Point, N. Y. Edwin and Alice Huntley live near Whitney Point, N. Y.

Ida Blair (d.), (m.) Alva Saddlemire, leaving three boys, Eugene, Clayton and Merton Saddlemire. Eugene (m.) Ethel Pollard. They have a daughter.

Clayton (m.) Miss Miner. They have a daughter. Merton is (m.)

Emma Della Blair has been three times married: First, Oliver Eldredge; second, Mr. Johnson. They had a daughter. Her third husband is Mr. Lowe.

Hattie Blair (m.) Mr. Schoolcraft. Two children, Arthur and Anita (d.) Hattie's second husband is Burley Lipe.

Luella Blair (m.) Amos Baldwin. Their children are: Eva, Lida, Pearl and Loren.

Lida, (m.) Mr. Dewey. Pearl (m.) Mr. Barr. These, with their mother live in Candor, N. Y. Loren Baldwin lives in Binghamton, N. Y.

For Oscar Blair record, see Eli Blair family, and for Mariette Blair see Dunn family.

Mahala Blair (d.), youngest of Joel Blair family, (m.) Ambrose Gray (d.) Their children are: Arthur, Frank, Etta, Gertrude, Eloise (d.), Nina and Virgie Gray.

Arthur (m.) Agnes Dennison (d.) Their children are: Otto, Arleigh, Clare, Zera, Gladys and a babe (d.) in infancy. Otto Gray (m.) Lillian Laithwait. One child. Home, Cranbrook, Canada.

Arleigh (m.) Allen Lamphere. One child, Dorothy. Home, Palouse, Washington.

Zera (m.) Gertrude Hart. Two children: Barbara Alicia, and a son. Home, Poulson, Montana.

Gladys Gray (m.) Andrew Burghardt. A son, Stanley Reese Burghardt. Home, Greene, N. Y. The third child, Clare Gray is unmarried.

Frank, son of Mahala Blair Gray (m.) Belle Madison. Home, Poulson, Mont.

Etta Gray (m.) Edwin Alderman. Home, Castle Creek, N. Y. One child, Luther, who (m.) Mamie Slack. One child, Wilma Alderman.

Gertrude Gray (m.) James Galloway. Three children: Dana, Harold (d.) and Robert. Home, Whitney Point, N. Y.

Nina Gray (m.) Frank Davis. One child, Irene Davis. Home, Whitney Point, N. Y.

Virgie Gray (m.) Harry Palmer. Two children: Helen and Lawrence Palmer. Home, Lydia Street, Binghamton, N. Y.

James Blair's youngest child was Polly, who (m.) Avery Cole. They had a son, Sewell Cole, (m.) Olive Walker. Their children were: Avery (b.) 1828, Mary and Roxie Cole. Avery

Cole (m.) Lovinia Gray. He (d.) 1910. Their children were: Charles, Ida and Louise Cole. Charles (m.) 1900, Jennie Cooper. He was a physician. They had one son, Avery Cole. Charles Cole (d.) 1916. Home, Edward Street, Binghamton, N. Y.

Ida Cole (m.) 1875, Zina Rockefeller. Their children are: Elmer, Amos Cole, Vinnie, Ernest, Adah and Raymond Rockefeller. Elmer (m.) Nettie Ozell. Two children: Percy and Selma Rockefeller. Amos (m.) Louella Ammerman. Two children: Ruth and Ralph Rockefeller. Vinnie (m.) Willis Brazee. One child, Belmore Brazee.

Louise, daughter of Avery Cole (m.) George Ross, 1895. Two children: George Marcus and Doris Ross. Home, 7 Edward Street, Binghamton, N. Y.

Mary, daughter of Sewell Cole (m.) Grandus Baker. Their children are: Sewell, Willis and Willet, twins, Frances, Josephine, Olive, Alberta and Bertha, twins, and Elmer and Elvin, twins. Mary Cole Baker (d.) as a comparatively young woman. Roxie, third child of Sewell Cole (m.) Pulaski Brown. One child, Libbie Brown (d.), (m.) Asa Tripp.

Milton Keynes UK
Ingram Content Group UK Ltd.
UKHW020618050324
438776UK00006B/936